THE
FEED YOUR HANGRY COOKBOOK

THE
FEED YOUR HANGRY
COOKBOOK

This book may be ordered by mail from the publisher. Please include $5.99 for postage and handling. Please support your local bookseller first!

Books published by Cider Mill Press Book Publishers are available at special discounts for bulk purchases in the United States by corporations, institutions, and other organizations. For more information, please contact the publisher.

Cider Mill Press Book Publishers
"Where good books are ready for press"

501 Nelson Place
Nashville, Tennessee 37214

cidermillpress.com

Typography: Bovine Round MVB, Acumin Pro, Interstate, Quasimoda.

Image Credits: Pages 19, 24, 36-37, 40, 43, 56-57, 58, 63, 73, 74, 78, 85, 86, 94, 97, 119, 122, 146, 160, 164, 167, and 180 courtesy of Cider Mill Press All other images used under official license from Shutterstock.com.

Printed in China

23 24 25 26 27 TYC 6 5 4 3 2

THE FEED YOUR HANGRY COOKBOOK

75+ Nutritious Recipes • to Keep Your Hunger in Check •

CIDER MILL PRESS

BOOK PUBLISHERS

CONTENTS

INTRODUCTION

Everyone knows what it's like to be hangry.

Your thinking gets cloudy. Every little thing starts to grate on you—whether it be an unexpected email, an innocent question from a friend, or a sound coming from the street. It feels as though the universe has focused all its energy on making you miserable, and your emotions become so outsized that it becomes tempting to just tear everything down, run away, and hide.

Worst of all, hanger can strike at any time—first thing in the morning, in the middle of a glorious afternoon, or late at night, when you shouldn't even be awake, never mind hungry. Because of this unpredictability, there's no one solution that's guaranteed to work—each occasion of hanger requires something different to soothe the pain.

Of course, no one wants this kind of trouble. But, in the course of modern life, it is inevitable that hanger will pop up on occasion. There is simply too much to do, too many options available, too many calls for our attention and energy to guarantee that one will always have a satisfying option at hand, never mind the desire to prepare it and clean up afterward.

Hanger may be inevitable, but we feel it's not something that should prove debilitating. It's simply something unpleasant that needs to be dealt with, like cold in the winter or taxes. Fortunately, hanger is far more fun to alleviate.

To make sure you can, no matter what your stomach is screaming for, we've scanned the globe and been hard at work in the kitchen to come up with an array of simple, delicious recipes that will set your inner house back in order. Sense hanger creeping up first thing in morning, threatening to submarine the rest of the day? A series of easy breakfast options keep you on track. Hanger pounding at the door, but you can't really afford to break from what you're doing? There's a host of quick, make-ahead snacks that are sure to satisfy. Had a long day that seems disastrous when put under the microscope of your hanger? Comforting classics will put things back in perspective. Got an entire crew of hangry folks who seem to be on the verge of tearing each other limb from limb? A dozen family-style, sit-down meals will quiet the crowd. And, if it's your sweet tooth that's clamoring for attention, there's also an assortment of decadent confections.

The next time hanger strikes, don't lose your head. Simply turn to this book, flip through until a solution presents itself, and enjoy the pleasant feeling of taking charge and sending misery packing.

IN THE
MORNING

There's never a good time to be hangry. But it's especially dangerous when hanger strikes first thing in the morning, as it threatens the entire day. This series of dishes ensures that you can navigate these turbulent times easily and set your house in order. Not only that, they'll provide the energy and sustenance to guarantee that hanger remains at bay for good.

AVOCADO TOAST

YIELD: **4 SERVINGS** / ACTIVE TIME: **10 MINUTES** / TOTAL TIME: **10 MINUTES**

INGREDIENTS

4 slices of thick-cut bacon

4 thick slices of sourdough bread

Flesh of 2 avocados

¼ cup full-fat Greek yogurt

Salt and pepper, to taste

DIRECTIONS

1   Place the bacon in a large skillet and cook over medium heat until it is crispy, about 8 minutes, turning the bacon as necessary. Transfer to a paper towel–lined plate to drain. When cool enough to handle, chop the bacon into bite-size pieces.

2   Using a toaster or your oven, toast the slices of bread.

3   While the bread is toasting, place the avocados and yogurt in a mixing bowl and mash until combined. Season the mixture with salt and pepper.

4   Spread the avocado mixture on the toast, top with the bacon, and enjoy.

HUEVOS RANCHEROS

YIELD: **4 SERVINGS** / ACTIVE TIME: **15 MINUTES** / TOTAL TIME: **20 MINUTES**

INGREDIENTS

¾ cup extra-virgin olive oil

4 corn tortillas

3 large tomatoes

¼ onion

2 serrano chile peppers, stems
and seeds removed, sliced

Salt, to taste

4 eggs

½ cup chopped fresh cilantro,
for garnish

8 oz. queso fresco, shredded,
for garnish

Black beans, for serving

DIRECTIONS

1 Place half the olive oil in a large skillet and warm over medium-high heat. Add the tortillas and fry for about 1 minute on each side. Transfer to a paper towel–lined plate and let them drain.

2 Place the tomatoes, onion, and chiles in a blender and puree until smooth.

3 Place 2 tablespoons of the remaining olive oil in a small skillet and warm over medium heat. Carefully add the puree, reduce the heat to low, and cook the salsa for 5 minutes. Season with salt and then set the salsa aside.

4 Place the remaining oil in a skillet, add the eggs, season the yolks generously with salt, and cook as desired.

5 To assemble, place an egg on top of a fried tortilla, spoon the salsa on top, and garnish with the cheese and cilantro. Serve with black beans.

HUEVOS RANCHEROS, see page 11

BUTTERMILK WAFFLES

YIELD: **4 SERVINGS** / ACTIVE TIME: **20 MINUTES** / TOTAL TIME: **30 MINUTES**

INGREDIENTS

2 cups all-purpose flour

2 tablespoons sugar

2 teaspoons baking powder

½ teaspoon kosher salt

2 cups buttermilk

8 tablespoons unsalted butter, melted

2 eggs

DIRECTIONS

1 Preheat a waffle iron. Place the flour, sugar, baking powder, and salt in a large bowl and whisk to combine.

2 Place the remaining ingredients in a separate mixing bowl, whisk to combine, and add the wet mixture to the dry mixture. Whisk until the mixture comes together as a smooth batter.

3 Pour the batter into the waffle iron and cook until browned and crispy.

BACON & ZUCCHINI FRITTATA

YIELD: **6 SERVINGS** / ACTIVE TIME: **10 MINUTES** / TOTAL TIME: **45 MINUTES**

INGREDIENTS

12 oz. thick-cut bacon, chopped

1 small zucchini, sliced

1 garlic clove, minced

4 oz. garlic & herb goat cheese

4 eggs

8 oz. baby spinach

1½ cups half-and-half

½ teaspoon kosher salt

½ teaspoon black pepper

DIRECTIONS

1 Preheat the oven to 350°F. Place the bacon in a 10-inch cast-iron skillet and cook over medium heat until crispy, about 10 minutes. Transfer the pieces to a paper towel–lined plate to drain.

2 Add the zucchini pieces and garlic to the skillet and cook until the zucchini has softened, about 6 minutes. Return the pieces of bacon to the skillet, add the goat cheese, and stir until evenly distributed.

3 Whisk the eggs until scrambled. Add the spinach, half-and-half, salt, and pepper, and whisk to combine. Pour the egg mixture into the skillet and shake the pan evenly to distribute.

4 Put the skillet in the oven and bake until the frittata is puffy and golden brown and the eggs are set, about 30 minutes. Remove from the oven and let the frittata sit for 5 minutes before slicing and serving.

PEANUT BUTTER & BACON OATS

YIELD: **6 SERVINGS** / ACTIVE TIME: **5 MINUTES** / TOTAL TIME: **20 MINUTES**

INGREDIENTS

6 slices of thick-cut bacon

6 eggs

2 cups steel-cut oats

6 cups water

1 tablespoon kosher salt

¼ cup crunchy peanut butter

DIRECTIONS

1 Place the bacon in a large cast-iron skillet and cook over medium heat until crispy, about 8 minutes. Transfer the bacon to a paper towel–lined plate, add the eggs to the skillet, and fry them in the bacon fat. Transfer the eggs to a plate and cover it loosely with aluminum foil to keep warm.

2 Wipe out the skillet, add the oats, water, and salt and cook over medium heat for 7 to 10 minutes, until the oats are tender.

3 While the oats are cooking, chop the bacon. Add the bacon and peanut butter to the oats and stir to incorporate. Ladle the oatmeal into warmed bowls, top each portion with a fried egg, and serve.

HAM & SWISS STRATA

YIELD: **4 SERVINGS** / ACTIVE TIME: **20 MINUTES** / TOTAL TIME: **1 HOUR**

INGREDIENTS

7 eggs

2 cups whole milk

4 oz. Swiss cheese, shredded

Pinch of freshly grated nutmeg

3 cups day-old bread pieces

1 cup diced leftover ham

1 yellow onion, minced

2 cups chopped fresh spinach

Salt and pepper, to taste

2 teaspoons extra-virgin olive oil

DIRECTIONS

1 Preheat the oven to 400°F. Place the eggs and milk in a large mixing bowl and whisk to combine. Add the cheese and nutmeg and stir to incorporate. Add the bread pieces and let the mixture sit for 10 minutes.

2 Add the ham, onion, and spinach to the egg-and-bread mixture and stir until evenly distributed. Season with salt and pepper.

3 Coat a 10-inch cast-iron skillet with the olive oil. Pour in the strata, place the skillet in the oven, and bake until it is golden brown and set in the center, about 25 minutes. Remove from the oven and let cool for 10 minutes before cutting into wedges and serving.

BLUEBERRY MUFFINS

YIELD: **12 MUFFINS** / ACTIVE TIME: **20 MINUTES** / TOTAL TIME: **1 HOUR**

INGREDIENTS

20 oz. all-purpose flour

1 tablespoon baking powder

1½ teaspoons kosher salt

8 oz. unsalted butter, softened

10 oz. sugar

6 eggs

½ cup sour cream

11 oz. milk

2 cups fresh blueberries

DIRECTIONS

1 Preheat the oven to 375°F and line a 12-well muffin pan with paper liners.

2 Place the flour, baking powder, and salt in a mixing bowl and whisk to combine. Set the mixture aside.

3 In the work bowl of a stand mixer fitted with the paddle attachment, cream the butter and sugar on medium until light and fluffy, about 5 minutes. Add the eggs and beat until incorporated. Add the dry mixture, reduce the speed to low, and beat until the mixture comes together as a smooth batter. Add the sour cream and beat until incorporated. Gradually add the milk and beat to incorporate. Add the blueberries, reduce the speed to low, and beat until evenly distributed.

4 Pour ½ cup of muffin batter into each liner. Place the pan in the oven and bake the muffins until a knife inserted into the center of each comes out clean, 20 to 25 minutes.

5 Remove from the oven, place the pan on a wire rack, and let the muffins cool completely before enjoying.

HAM & CHEESE CROISSANTS

YIELD: **16 CROISSANTS** / ACTIVE TIME: **30 MINUTES** / TOTAL TIME: **2 HOURS**

INGREDIENTS

1 sheet of frozen puff
pastry, thawed

⅔ cup Dijon mustard

16 slices of smoked ham

16 slices of Swiss cheese

1 egg, beaten

DIRECTIONS

1 Preheat the oven to 400°F and line two baking sheets with parchment paper. Roll out the sheet of puff pastry until it is very thin. Using a pizza cutter or a chef's knife, cut the puff pastry into rectangles, and then cut each rectangle diagonally, yielding 16 triangles. Gently roll out each triangle until it is 8 inches long.

2 Spread 2 teaspoons of the mustard toward the wide side of each triangle. Lay a slice of ham over the mustard and top it with a slice of cheese, making sure to leave 1 inch of dough uncovered at the tip.

3 Roll the croissants up tight, moving from the wide side of the triangle to the tip. Tuck the tips under the croissants. Place eight croissants on each of the baking sheets.

4 Place the croissants in the oven and bake until they are golden brown, 20 to 22 minutes. Remove the croissants from the oven and place them on wire racks. Let the croissants cool slightly before enjoying.

MIDDAY
MUNCHIES

Maybe you've got so much work that you didn't get a chance to eat lunch. Maybe you did have lunch, but it's not doing the trick. Whatever the reason for your afternoon hanger, it's essential that you be able to calm it with a quick bite. This collection of make-ahead preparations and speedy snacks guarantees that you don't get knocked off track near the finish line, helping you power through and keep what's left of your patience.

CAPRESE SALAD

YIELD: **4 SERVINGS** / ACTIVE TIME: **15 MINUTES** / TOTAL TIME: **15 MINUTES**

INGREDIENTS

1 lb. in-season heirloom
tomatoes, sliced

Salt and pepper, to taste

1 lb. fresh mozzarella
cheese, sliced

¼ cup pesto

Quality extra-virgin olive oil,
to taste

DIRECTIONS

1 Season the tomatoes with salt and pepper. While alternating, arrange them and the slices of mozzarella on a platter.

2 Drizzle the pesto and olive oil over the tomatoes and mozzarella and serve.

SPANISH TORTILLA

YIELD: **6 SERVINGS** / ACTIVE TIME: **30 MINUTES** / TOTAL TIME: **2 HOURS**

INGREDIENTS

5 large russet potatoes, peeled and sliced thin

1 Spanish onion, sliced

½ cup canola oil, plus more as needed

½ cup extra-virgin olive oil

10 eggs, at room temperature

Large pinch of kosher salt

DIRECTIONS

1   Place the potatoes, onion, canola oil, and olive oil in a 12-inch cast-iron skillet. The potatoes should be submerged. If not, add more vegetable oil as needed. Bring to a gentle simmer over low heat and cook until the potatoes are tender, about 30 minutes. Remove from heat and let cool slightly.

2   Use a slotted spoon to remove the potatoes and onion from the oil. Reserve the oil. Place the eggs and salt in a large bowl and whisk to combine. Add the potatoes and onion to the eggs.

3   Warm the skillet over high heat. Add ¼ cup of the reserved oil and swirl to coat the bottom and sides of the pan. Pour the egg-and-potato mixture into the pan and stir vigorously to ensure that the mixture does not stick to the sides. Cook for 1 minute and remove from heat. Place the pan over low heat, cover, and cook for 3 minutes.

4   Carefully invert the tortilla onto a large plate. Return it to the skillet, cook for 3 minutes, and then invert it onto the plate. Return it to the skillet and cook for another 3 minutes. Remove the tortilla from the pan and let it rest at room temperature for 1 hour before serving.

BREAD & BUTTER PICKLES

YIELD: ½ CUP / ACTIVE TIME: **5 MINUTES** / TOTAL TIME: **24 HOURS**

INGREDIENTS

2 Persian cucumbers, sliced thin

1 small onion, sliced thin

2 jalapeño chile peppers, sliced thin

4 sprigs of fresh dill

2 tablespoons coriander seeds

2 tablespoons mustard seeds

2 teaspoons celery salt

2 cups distilled white vinegar

½ cup sugar

2 tablespoons kosher salt

DIRECTIONS

1 Place the cucumbers, onion, jalapeños, dill, coriander seeds, mustard seeds, and celery salt in a 1-quart mason jar.

2 Place the vinegar, sugar, and salt in a medium saucepan and bring it to a boil, stirring to dissolve the sugar and salt. Carefully pour the brine into jar, filling all the way to the top. If you want to can these pickles, see the sidebar on the opposite page. If you do not want to can the pickles, let the mixture cool completely before sealing and storing in the refrigerator, where they will keep for up to 1 week.

INGREDIENTS

9 oz. all-purpose flour

1.8 oz. cocoa powder

1½ teaspoons baking soda

½ teaspoon kosher salt

4 oz. unsalted butter, softened

8 oz. sugar

1 egg

1 teaspoon pure vanilla extract

1 cup buttermilk

2 cups marshmallow creme

VANILLA PUDDING

YIELD: **8 SERVINGS** / ACTIVE TIME: **20 MINUTES** / TOTAL TIME: **2 HOURS AND 20 MINUTES**

INGREDIENTS

3 large egg yolks

⅓ cup sugar

2 tablespoons cornstarch

¼ teaspoon fine sea salt

2 cups whole milk

2 tablespoons unsalted butter, softened

2 tablespoons pure vanilla extract

DIRECTIONS

1   Place the egg yolks in a bowl and beat until combined.

2   Place the sugar, cornstarch, and salt in a saucepan, stir to combine, and warm over medium heat. Slowly add the milk and whisk constantly as the mixture comes to a simmer.

3   Remove the saucepan from heat and, whisking continually, add approximately one-third of the warm mixture into the beaten egg yolks. Pour the tempered egg yolks into the saucepan, place it back over medium heat, and cook for 1 minute while stirring constantly. Remove the pan from heat.

4   Stir in the butter and vanilla. Transfer the pudding into serving dishes and place plastic wrap directly on the surface of each one to prevent a skin from forming. Place the pudding in the refrigerator and chill for 2 hours before enjoying.

PEPPERMINT BARK

YIELD: **24 SERVINGS** / ACTIVE TIME: **15 MINUTES** / TOTAL TIME: **1 HOUR**

INGREDIENTS

¾ cup crushed peppermint candies

12 oz. semisweet chocolate chips

2 teaspoons canola oil

12 oz. white chocolate chips

DIRECTIONS

1 Line a rimmed baking sheet with parchment paper and place the crushed peppermint candies in a mixing bowl.

2 Fill a small saucepan halfway with water and bring it to a gentle simmer. Place the semisweet chocolate chips in a heatproof bowl, place it over the simmering water, and stir until melted. Keep the water at a simmer.

3 Stir 1 teaspoon of the canola oil into the melted chocolate and then pour the chocolate onto the baking sheet, using a rubber spatula to distribute evenly. Place the baking sheet in the refrigerator until the chocolate has set, about 30 minutes.

4 Place the white chocolate chips in a heatproof bowl, place it over the simmering water, and stir until melted. Stir in the remaining canola oil and pour the melted white chocolate on top of the hardened semisweet chocolate, using a rubber spatula to distribute evenly.

5 Sprinkle the peppermint pieces liberally over the white chocolate and press down on them lightly. Refrigerate until the white chocolate is set, about 30 minutes. Break the bark into pieces and refrigerate until ready to serve.

CARAMEL POPCORN

YIELD: **4 SERVINGS** / ACTIVE TIME: **15 MINUTES** / TOTAL TIME: **45 MINUTES**

INGREDIENTS

1 bag of microwave popcorn

6 tablespoons unsalted butter

⅓ cup light corn syrup

½ cup light brown sugar

½ cup sugar

¼ teaspoon kosher salt

¼ teaspoon pure vanilla extract

DIRECTIONS

1 Pop the bag of popcorn in the microwave and set aside. Line a baking sheet with parchment paper and coat it with nonstick cooking spray.

2 In a large saucepan fitted with a candy thermometer, combine the butter, corn syrup, brown sugar, sugar, and salt and cook over medium heat, swirling the pan occasionally, until the caramel reaches 248°F.

3 Whisk in the vanilla, add the bag of popcorn, and fold the mixture until the caramel is evenly distributed.

4 Transfer the caramel popcorn to the baking sheet and spread it into an even layer. Let cool completely before enjoying.

CHOCOLATE CHIP COOKIES

YIELD: **16 COOKIES** / ACTIVE TIME: **15 MINUTES** / TOTAL TIME: **45 MINUTES**

INGREDIENTS

7 oz. unsalted butter

8¾ oz. all-purpose flour

½ teaspoon baking soda

3½ oz. sugar

5 1/3 oz. dark brown sugar

1 teaspoon fine sea salt

2 teaspoons pure vanilla extract

1 large egg

1 large egg yolk

1¼ cups semisweet chocolate chips

DIRECTIONS

1 Preheat the oven to 350°F. Place the butter in a saucepan and cook over medium-high heat until it is starting to brown and give off a nutty aroma (let your nose guide you here, making sure you frequently waft the steam toward you). Transfer to a heatproof mixing bowl.

2 Place the flour and baking soda in a bowl and whisk until combined.

3 Add the sugars, salt, and vanilla to the bowl containing the melted butter and whisk until combined. Add the egg and egg yolk and whisk until mixture is smooth and thick. Add the flour-and-baking soda mixture and stir until incorporated. Add the chocolate chips and stir until evenly distributed. Form the mixture into 16 balls and place on parchment-lined baking sheets, leaving about 2 inches between each ball.

4 Working with one baking sheet at a time, place it in the oven and bake until golden brown, 12 to 16 minutes, rotating the sheet halfway through the bake time. Remove from the oven and let cool to room temperature before serving.

COCONUT MACAROONS

YIELD: **12 MACAROONS** / ACTIVE TIME: **45 MINUTES** / TOTAL TIME: **3 HOURS**

INGREDIENTS

1 (14 oz.) can of sweetened condensed milk

7 oz. sweetened shredded coconut

7 oz. unsweetened shredded coconut

¼ teaspoon kosher salt

½ teaspoon pure vanilla extract

2 egg whites

2 oz. chocolate, melted

DIRECTIONS

1 Line an 18 x 13–inch baking sheet with parchment paper. In a mixing bowl, add the sweetened condensed milk, shredded coconut, salt, and vanilla and stir with a rubber spatula until combined. Set the mixture aside.

2 In the work bowl of a stand mixer fitted with the whisk attachment, whip the egg whites until they hold stiff peaks. Add the whipped egg whites to the coconut mixture and fold to incorporate.

3 Scoop 2-oz. portions of the mixture onto a baking sheet, making sure to leave enough space between them. Place the baking sheet in the refrigerator and let the dough firm up for 1 hour.

4 Preheat the oven to 350°F.

5 Place the cookies in the oven and bake until they are lightly golden brown, 20 to 25 minutes.

6 Remove the cookies from the oven, transfer them to a cooling rack, and let them cool for 1 hour.

7 Dip the bottoms of the macaroons into the melted chocolate and then place them back on the baking sheet. If desired, drizzle some of the chocolate over the tops of the cookies. Refrigerate until the chocolate is set, about 5 minutes, before serving.

HONEY NUT TRUFFLES

YIELD: **16 TRUFFLES** / ACTIVE TIME: **10 MINUTES** / TOTAL TIME: **2 HOURS**

INGREDIENTS

½ cup peanut butter

¼ cup honey

¼ teaspoon kosher salt

1 cup chopped high-quality chocolate

DIRECTIONS

1   Place the peanut butter, honey, and salt in a bowl and stir until well combined. Form teaspoons of the mixture into balls, place them on a parchment-lined baking sheet, and refrigerate for 1 hour.

2   Remove the baking sheet from the refrigerator. Bring water to a simmer in a medium saucepan and place the chocolate in a heatproof mixing bowl. Place the bowl over the simmering water and stir the chocolate occasionally until it is melted.

3   Dip the balls into the melted chocolate until completely coated. Place them back on the baking sheet. When all the truffles have been coated, place them in the refrigerator and chill until the chocolate is set.

CHOCOLATE-DIPPED STRAWBERRIES

YIELD: **8 SERVINGS** / ACTIVE TIME: **10 MINUTES** / TOTAL TIME: **2 HOURS AND 10 MINUTES**

INGREDIENTS

2 pints of fresh strawberries

2 cups dark chocolate chips

DIRECTIONS

1 Rinse the strawberries well and pat them dry.

2 Fill a small saucepan halfway with water and bring it to a simmer. Place the chocolate chips in a heatproof bowl and place it over the simmering water. Stir occasionally until the chocolate is melted.

3 Dip each strawberry into the chocolate halfway, or completely, whichever you prefer. Line a baking sheet with parchment paper and place the strawberries on the sheet. Place in the refrigerator and chill for at least 2 hours before serving.

MUDDY BUDDIES

YIELD: **8 TO 10 SERVINGS** / ACTIVE TIME: **5 MINUTES** / TOTAL TIME: **50 MINUTES**

INGREDIENTS

1 cup semisweet chocolate chips

¾ cup creamy peanut butter

1 teaspoon pure vanilla extract

9 cups Rice Chex

1½ cups confectioners' sugar

DIRECTIONS

1 Place the chocolate chips and peanut butter in a microwave-safe bowl and microwave on medium for 30 seconds. Remove from the microwave, add the vanilla, and stir until the mixture is smooth.

2 Place the Chex in a large mixing bowl and pour the peanut butter-and-chocolate mixture over the cereal. Carefully stir until all of the Chex are coated.

3 Place the mixture into a large resealable plastic bag and add the confectioners' sugar. Seal bag and shake until each piece of Chex is coated with sugar.

4 Pour the mixture onto a parchment-lined baking sheet and refrigerate for 45 minutes before serving.

DARK CHOCOLATE & STOUT BROWNIES

YIELD: **16 BROWNIES** / ACTIVE TIME: **15 MINUTES** / TOTAL TIME: **1 HOUR AND 15 MINUTES**

INGREDIENTS

8 oz. unsalted butter, plus more as needed

12 oz. Guinness

12 oz. dark chocolate chips

1½ cups sugar

3 large eggs

1 teaspoon pure vanilla extract

¾ cup all-purpose flour

1¼ teaspoons kosher salt

Cocoa powder, as needed

DIRECTIONS

1   Preheat the oven to 350°F and coat a square 8-inch cake pan with butter. Place the Guinness in a saucepan and bring to a boil. Cook until it has reduced by half. Remove the pan from heat and let it cool.

2   Bring water to a boil in a saucepan. Place the chocolate chips and the butter in a heatproof bowl, place it over the simmering water, and stir until the mixture is smooth.

3   Place the sugar, eggs, and vanilla in a large bowl and stir until combined. Slowly whisk in the chocolate-and-butter mixture and then whisk in the stout.

4   Add the flour and salt and fold to incorporate. Pour batter into greased pan, place in the oven, and bake for 35 to 40 minutes, until the surface begins to crack and a toothpick inserted in the center comes out with a just few moist crumbs attached.

5   Remove the brownies from the oven, place the pan on a wire rack, and let cool for at least 20 minutes. When cool, sprinkle the cocoa powder over the top and cut the brownies into squares.

METRIC CONVERSIONS

U.S. Measurement	Approximate Metric Liquid Measurement	Approximate Metric Dry Measurement
1 teaspoon	5 ml	5 g
1 tablespoon or ½ ounce	15 ml	14 g
1 ounce or ⅛ cup	30 ml	29 g
¼ cup or 2 ounces	60 ml	57 g
⅓ cup	80 ml	76 g
½ cup or 4 ounces	120 ml	113 g
⅔ cup	160 ml	151 g
¾ cup or 6 ounces	180 ml	170 g
1 cup or 8 ounces or ½ pint	240 ml	227 g
1½ cups or 12 ounces	350 ml	340 g
2 cups or 1 pint or 16 ounces	475 ml	454 g
3 cups or 1½ pints	700 ml	680 g
4 cups or 2 pints or 1 quart	950 ml	908 g

INDEX

ABOUT CIDER MILL PRESS BOOK PUBLISHERS

Good ideas ripen with time. From seed to harvest, Cider Mill Press brings fine reading, information, and entertainment together between the covers of its creatively crafted books. Our Cider Mill bears fruit twice a year, publishing a new crop of titles each spring and fall.

"WHERE GOOD BOOKS ARE READY FOR PRESS"

501 Nelson Place
Nashville, Tennessee 37214

cidermillpress.com